20 Answers

Homosexuality

Jim Blackburn

Catholic
Answers
Press

20 Answers: Homosexuality

Jim Blackburn

© 2017 Catholic Answers

Published by Catholic Answers, Inc.

2020 Gillespie Way

El Cajon, California 92020

1-888-291-8000 orders

619-387-0042 fax

catholic.com

Printed in the United States of America

978-1-68357-033-2

978-1-68357-034-9 Kindle

978-1-68357-035-6 ePub

Introduction

Homosexuality is a controversial topic that has relatively recently raced to the forefront of cultural and political concerns worldwide. Catholics and other Christians have been forced into the spotlight on these issues with charges of being "on the wrong side of history." Our witness in this regard must be firm and articulate yet respectful, compassionate, and sensitive.

In this booklet we will explore precisely what the Catholic Church teaches about same-sex attraction and homosexuality. We will look at what the Bible says about these matters and refute modern activists' self-serving reinterpretations of Scripture. These include such claims as the sin of Sodom and Gomorrah being mere inhospitality, Jesus' apparent silence about homosexuality being tacit approval of it, and St. Paul's clear condemnations amounting to misogynistic bigotry. We will also examine why Catholics sometimes are accused of cherry-picking from the Old Testament laws.

Several answers in the following pages concern direct challenges Catholics face from homosexuality-supporting activists and the people who learn from them. It is common today for such people to attack Catholic teaching and to shame us over to their side of the argument. These include accusations that we are equivalent to racist bigots, that we are judgmental and intolerant, and that we are hateful people who do not follow Christ's true message of love.

Additionally, we will examine the modern inventions of so-called "gay marriage" and other forms of same-sex unions, as well as consider the prospect of whether or not to attend a "gay wedding," a challenge Catholics increasingly face today.

Finally, we will look at ways to help people who have loved ones who experience same-sex attractions as well as ways to help people who themselves experience same-sex attractions.

1. What is homosexuality?

To understand homosexuality, it helps to first understand sexuality in general.

Sexuality is part of our natural makeup to desire sexual gratification. Mankind was created with sexual desires, and it is consistent with God's plan for us to engage in sexual relations open to procreation within marriage.

Jesus said,

Have you not read that he who made them from the beginning made them male and female, and said, "For this reason a man shall leave his father and mother and be joined to his wife, and the two shall become one flesh"? So they are no longer two but one flesh. What therefore God has joined together, let not man put asunder (Matt. 19:4–6).

For most people, the drive to fulfill sexual desire is inclined toward the opposite sex. So long as one morally confines it to within his own marriage, sexual activity is ordered toward good. The *Catechism of the Catholic Church* (CCC) states, "Sexuality is ordered to the conjugal love of man and woman. In marriage, the physical intimacy of the spouses becomes a sign and pledge of spiritual communion. Marriage bonds between baptized persons are sanctified by the sacrament" (CCC 2360).

Therefore, sexuality properly ordered is a beautiful gift from God that impacts our entire lives: "*Sexuality* affects all aspects of the human person in the unity of his body and soul. It especially concerns affectivity, the capacity to love and to procreate, and in a more general way the aptitude for forming bonds of communion with others" (CCC 2332).

Tragically, for reasons not fully understood, some people experience a disordered sexual desire inclined toward the same sex. These desires themselves are not sinful, but they are a temptation to sin. The *Catechism* calls such temptation *concupiscence* (CCC 405). Concupiscence inclines us to commit sin, but with God's help, we can resist it. On the other hand, sexual *activity* between persons of the same sex is immoral, and thus, when freely and knowingly chosen, it is sinful.

The Church recognizes that this is no small issue: "The number of men and women who have deep-seated homosexual tendencies is not negligible" (CCC 2358). In recent decades, the topic of homosexuality has become prominent not only within the Church, but in secular society as well. The Church has devoted substantial time and effort to teaching the world what God wants us to know about sexuality, marriage, and homosexuality.

2. What does the Church teach about homosexuality?

The *Catechism of the Catholic Church* teaches,

> Basing itself on Sacred Scripture, which presents homosexual acts as acts of grave depravity, tradition has always declared that homosexual acts are intrinsically disordered. They are contrary to the natural law. They close the sexual act to the gift of life. They do not proceed from a genuine affective and sexual complementarity. Under no circumstances can they be approved (CCC 2357; *Persona Humana* 8).

First, homosexual acts are intrinsically disordered. This means that such acts are never ordered toward a moral purpose. Sexual activity, to be morally ordered, must always take place only in the context of a conjugal act between a husband and his wife.

Next, homosexual acts are contrary to the natural law. The natural law is the body of knowledge humanity can grasp by the aid of reason alone. It is the basis for much of our moral understanding. For example, we know almost intuitively that lying, stealing, and murdering are seriously immoral actions. Similarly, we know that our bodies are designed naturally to fit together male with female, not in an unnatural homosexual way.

Homosexual acts close the sexual act to the gift of life. In other words, such acts are not ordered toward their natural end: procreation. Indeed, homosexual acts, by their nature, can never fulfill this basic function so necessary to the survival of humanity.

Homosexual acts do not proceed from a genuine affective and sexual complementarity. Men and women are different, and this can be seen both in how we relate to one another and in how we engage in sexual activity together. Human bodies are made male and female in a complementary design necessary for the propagation of our species. To engage in sexual activity with any type of partner other than a member of the opposite sex—be it a person of the same sex, an animal, or an inanimate object—is contrary to the complementarity of physical design. (For more on this, see Answers 14–17.)

Because of all this, homosexual activity can never be approved. To do so is gravely contrary to God's plan for us. It is sinful. We are all called to be God's children, and in order to be so, we must reject sin.

Homosexual desires, inasmuch as they are *passions*, which we do not choose, are not in themselves sinful. We all have attraction to sin—desires to do things we are not supposed to do. Such is the condition of our fallen human nature, corrupted by original sin.

The Church does not claim to know the scientific or biological reasons behind homosexuality (CCC 2357; see also Answer 9), but knowledge of such information is irrelevant in light of the fact that Scripture and the natural law tell us that homosexual activity—behavior that is chosen, even if the desire for it is not—is always immoral. People tempted by same-sex attractions—like people tempted by any other sinful desire—do not sin unless they act on them: whether in sexual activity or in willfully entertaining lustful thoughts. Such temptations must be resisted. The Church teaches this while recognizing that a substantial number of people suffer from same-sex attractions and that we need to treat them like anyone else who is attracted to sin. Thus, the *Catechism* states:

The number of men and women who have deep-seated homosexual tendencies is not negligible. This inclination, which is objectively disordered, constitutes for most of them a trial. They must be accepted with respect, compassion, and sensitivity. Every sign of unjust discrimination in their regard should be avoided. These persons are called to fulfill God's will in their lives and, if they are Christians, to unite to the sacrifice of the Lord's cross the difficulties they may encounter from their condition (CCC 2358; see also Answer 19).

In other words, people with same-sex attractions should see these attractions as a test. To pass the test (i.e., to avoid sin), they must resist acting on the desires. This means being chaste. The virtue of *chastity* is the right ordering and use of our sexuality according to our state of life.

The *Catechism* states, "Homosexual persons are called to chastity. By the virtues of self-mastery that teach them inner freedom, at times by the support of disinterested friendship, by prayer and sacramental grace, they can and should gradually and resolutely approach Christian perfection" (CCC 2359).

Persons with same-sex attractions are called to the same moral standard as people with heterosexual desires: sexual activity outside authentic marriage is immoral for anyone and everyone. Someone with heterosexual desires may experience lust for someone other than his spouse, but to revel in or seek to fulfill that lust is unchaste.

The Church, obedient to the Lord who founded her and gave to her the sacramental life, celebrates the divine plan of the loving and live-giving union of men and women in the sacrament of marriage. It is only in the marital relationship that the use of the sexual faculty can be morally good. A person engaging in homosexual behavior therefore acts immorally (*Letter to the Bishops of the Catholic Church on the Pastoral Care of Homosexual Persons* 7).

3. What does the Bible teach about homosexuality?

Both the Old and New Testaments condemn homosexual activity whenever it is mentioned. There are six main passages, three in each Testament, where such behavior is explicitly addressed.

It doesn't take long to find the first condemnation of homosexual activity in the Old Testament. It is brought up in the very first book of the Bible, in the story of the destruction of Sodom and Gomorrah (Gen. 18–19). After Abraham and his wife Sarah are visited by angels and promised a son, the angels depart for the cities of Sodom and Gomorrah to see whether or not the outcry against the residents of those cities is justified, "because the outcry against Sodom and Gomorrah is great and their sin is very grave" (Gen. 18:20). Abraham's nephew Lot and his family are living in Sodom at the time, and they offer the angels accommodations for the night.

After dinner, just before bedtime, a mob surrounds the house and demands that the angels, thought to be men, be turned over to the men of the city for their homosexual pleasure. (For more details on the sin of Sodom and Gomorrah, see Answer 2.) Their aggressive demand seems to confirm for the angels that the outcry against the cities is, indeed, justified, so they destroy the cities the next morning after allowing Lot and his family to escape.

This may be the best known and most discussed Bible passage concerning God's condemnation of homosexual activity. Such activity is identified here as a grave sin, and the men involved in it lose their lives as a consequence of their actions.

In addition to this story, the Old Testament explicitly deals with homosexuality two more times.

After their exodus from Egypt, while still wandering in the desert, the Israelites receive the Law from Moses as God has delivered it to him. Among the laws laid down, God commands the Israelites, "You shall not lie with a male as with a woman; it is an abomination" (Lev. 18:22). He then institutes the death penalty for disobeying this commandment: "If a man lies with a male as with a woman, both of them have committed an abomination; they shall be put to death, their blood is upon them" (Lev. 20:13). The death penalty does not apply in most civil societies today (see Answer 5), but the fact that it applied in this case in ancient Israel clearly shows God's strong disapproval of homosexual activity.

All three explicit mentions of homosexual activity in the New Testament come from St. Paul. (It is sometimes noted as significant that the New Testament authors never record Jesus explicitly addressing homosexual activity. This issue is considered in Answer 6.) St. Paul calls homosexual activity "unnatural" and points out that it has serious consequences: "Women exchanged natural relations for unnatural, and the men likewise gave up natural relations with women and were consumed with passion for one another, men committing shameless acts with men and receiving in their own persons the due penalty for their error" (Rom. 1:26–27).

Serious Scripture scholars have always recognized Paul's clear references to homosexual desire and activity in this passage as well as Paul's blanket condemnation of all such activity. But some people attempt to reinterpret Paul's words here, arguing that his mention of "unnatural" relations should be understood to mean only homosexual relations between persons who are not same-sex-attracted, and that only those such actions are condemned. According to this argument, homosexual relations among persons *with same-sex attractions* are not unnatural, so Paul does not condemn them. This assertion is easily refuted, since Paul speaks of men being "consumed with passion for one another," which indicates desire—in this context, homosexual desire.

The men are clearly same-sex-attracted. This is not to say that homosexual activity among other persons is not also unnatural and condemned; indeed, it is. But if Paul had been talking about men *without* same-sex attractions in this passage, he would not have characterized them as being "consumed with passion" for one another, as this phrase implies homosexual desire.

In his first letter to the Corinthians, Paul clarifies that the penalty for homosexual activity (as well as some other sins) is the loss of salvation: "do you not know that the unrighteous will not inherit the kingdom of God? Do not be deceived; neither the immoral, nor idolaters, nor adulterers, nor homosexuals, nor thieves, nor the greedy, nor drunkards, nor revilers, nor robbers will inherit the kingdom of God" (1 Cor. 6:9–10). The phrase "nor homosexuals" is translated here from Greek text (*oute malakoi oute arsenokoitai*) that implies homosexual activity, not simply homosexual desire.

With Paul's mention also of adulterers, we see that people with same-sex attractions are called to the same standard as people with naturally ordered desires: sexual activity outside marriage is immoral for anyone and everyone.

Finally, Paul writes, "The law is not laid down for the just but for the lawless and disobedient, for the ungodly and sinners, for the unholy and profane, for murderers of fathers and murderers of mothers, for manslayers, immoral persons, sodomites, kidnappers, liars, perjurers, and whatever else is contrary to sound doctrine" (1 Tim. 1:9–10). The term *sodomites* used here is translated from Greek text meaning males engaging in sexual activity with other males. This is not lost on the translators, who relate such activity to the sin of Sodom.

4. Wasn't the sin of Sodom inhospitality, not homosexuality?

Some people—especially activists who wish to normalize homosexual activity—claim that Sodom was destroyed for being inhospitable and not for homosexual activity. This type of modern biblical re-interpretation is an issue the Church has found it necessary to address. For example, the Congregation for the Doctrine of the Faith explains in its *Letter to the Bishops of the Catholic Church on the Pastoral Care of Homosexual Persons* (CHP):

> An essential dimension of authentic pastoral care is the identification of causes of confusion regarding the Church's teaching. One is a new exegesis of Sacred Scripture which claims variously that Scripture has nothing to say on the subject of homosexuality, or that it somehow tacitly approves of it, or that all of its moral injunctions are so culture-bound that they are no longer applicable to contemporary life. These

views are gravely erroneous and call for particular attention here . . .

There is nevertheless a clear consistency within Scripture itself on the moral issue of homosexual behavior. The Church's doctrine regarding this issue is thus based, not on isolated phrases for facile theological argument, but on the solid foundation of a constant biblical testimony. The community of faith today, in unbroken continuity with the Jewish and Christian communities within which the ancient scriptures were written, continues to be nourished by those same scriptures and by the spirit of truth, whose word they are. It is likewise essential to recognize that the scriptures are not properly understood when they are interpreted in a way which contradicts the Church's living Tradition. To be correct, the interpretation of Scripture must be in substantial accord with that Tradition (CHP 4–5).

Certainly, the sins of Sodom included inhospitality (among many others that could be named), but the scriptural and historical understanding of both Judaism and Christianity is that the Sodomites' grave sin, which cried out to heaven (Gen. 18:21; 19:13), is the sin of homosexual activity.

The angels are sent to Sodom to observe the townsmen's behavior to see if the outcry over their grave sin is justified. The men of Sodom demand that the angels be turned over to them so that they may *know* (Hebrew, *yodu*) them. The term "know" is often used in Scripture (and elsewhere) as a euphemism for sexual activity. In this episode, it becomes clear that the townsmen's demand is meant to be understood in the homosexual context, as they refuse Lot's offer of his two daughters. His daughters are described as women who have *not* "known" men. In other words, they have never had sex; they are virgins. The townsmen refuse Lot's offer (thankfully for the women), because they want to know only the men whom Lot is housing. Their desire to sexually know the men obviously is homosexually inclined. It is this grave action toward the angels that convinces them that the outcry against Sodom is justified.

A similar narrative is related in Judges 19. In this case, the demanding townsmen of Gibeah do not refuse a concubine who is put outside for them, and by morning, she has been raped to death. Though the similarities between the two narratives are undeniable, it is significant to recognize that the townsmen of Sodom refused women as an alternative. Their desires were unquestionably homosexual in nature.

When arguing that the grave sin (Gen. 18:20) of Sodom was simply inhospitality, proponents often cite Ezekiel, who mentions that the Sodomites "did not aid the poor and needy" (Ezek. 16:49). This was clearly inhospitable behavior, but Ezekiel goes on to say that Sodom also committed "abominable things"

(Ezek. 16:50), which seems to refer to sexual acts of sin (clearly homosexual, given the context). So homosexual acts and inhospitality both may have contributed to the destruction of Sodom, but it is the former that is more consistently seen as the far worse sin—the grave sin that cries out to heaven.

In the New Testament, St. Peter describes the grave sin of Sodom as "licentiousness" (2 Pet. 2:7; Greek, *aselgeia*), which implies sexual unrestraint, homosexual in the given context. Similarly, Jude explains that Sodom was destroyed because the inhabitants "acted immorally and indulged in unnatural lust" (Jude 1:7). Again, we might see more than one sin referenced here, but it cannot be denied that homosexual activity is mentioned, since the men indulged in "unnatural [homosexual] lust."

Beyond Scripture, Jewish and Christian scholars have recognized that the primary sin of Sodom was its townsmen's homosexual activity. Indeed, the term *sodomy* has come to refer to the types of sexual activity engaged in by males with same-sex attractions.

Space does not permit an exhaustive treatment of the historical scholarship on this topic, but a few brief examples spanning the lengthy history of the Church should suffice. In the late sixth or early seventh century, bishop and Bible commentator Oecumenius wrote, "The unnatural lust in which the Sodomites indulged was homosexuality" (*Commentary on Jude*). Similarly, the *Douay Catechism of 1649* identifies one of the sins that cries out to heaven for vengeance as "the sin of Sodom, or carnal sin against nature, which is a voluntary shedding of the seed of nature, out of the due use of marriage, or lust with a different sex [from the one ordered by nature]" (Chapter XX; see also CCC 1867). In other words, the grave sin of Sodom is a sexual sin—homosexual, given the context. Finally, the CDF in 1986 taught, "In Genesis 19:1–11, the deterioration due to sin continues in the story of the men of Sodom. There can be no doubt of the moral judgment made there against homosexual relations" (CHP 6).

Thus, although the sins of Sodom were many, homosexual activity stands out as their grave sin that cried out to heaven.

5. Why do Catholics follow Old Testament teaching on homosexuality but not on other issues?

People sometimes ask, "Since we agree with Old Testament condemnations on homosexual activity, why do we not hold to other Old Testament laws as well?" For example, why do Christians relax the laws on eating pork when the Old Testament prohibits it (Lev. 11:7)? The point is this: since Christians do not follow *all* of the laws found in the Old Testament, it doesn't make sense that we expect anyone to observe Old Testament laws on homosexuality. The Old Testament is rendered irrelevant.

On the other hand, people sometimes take an opposite approach to Old Testament law, claiming that Christians *should* follow all of it rigidly. This approach is prevalent among Christians who insist that we worship on Saturday, the Sabbath, because this is commanded in the Old Testament. They argue that the early Church had no authority to designate Sunday as the primary Christian day of worship when God explicitly set aside Saturday for that purpose.

With all this confusion, what are we to do? Ignore all Old Testament laws? Observe all of them? Pick and choose? The answer is none of the above.

Old Testament law, of itself, is not binding on Christians. It never has been. In fact, it was only ever binding on those to whom it was delivered: the Jews (Israelites). Jesus fulfills that law: "Think not that I have come to abolish the Law and the prophets; I have come not to abolish them but to fulfill them" (Matt. 5:17). How can Jesus fulfill the Old Law without abolishing it?

The *Catechism* states, "Man is invited to rediscover [the Law] in the person of his Master who is its perfect fulfillment" (CCC 2053).

Consider the old dietary laws (e.g., regarding eating pork, as mentioned above). Jesus discusses such laws: "'Do you not see that whatever goes into a man from outside cannot defile him, since it enters, not his heart but his stomach, and so passes on?' (Thus he declared all foods clean)" (Mark 7:14–19). The *Catechism* explains,

"Jesus perfects the dietary law, so important in Jewish daily life, by revealing its pedagogical meaning through a divine interpretation. . . . What comes out of a man is what defiles a man. For from within, out of the heart of man, come evil thoughts" (CCC 582). Regarding Sabbath worship, Jesus indicates that he—not the Old Law—has authority over the Sabbath (Matt. 12:1–8). After the Resurrection, regulation of *when* to worship became the domain of the Church (see Answer 8), and corporate worship was moved to Sunday. Paul teaches similarly: "Let no one pass judgment on you in questions of food and drink or with regard to a festival or a new moon or a Sabbath. These are only a shadow of what is to come; but the substance belongs to Christ" (Col. 2:16–17).

There are elements of the natural law contained in Old Testament law, and these laws must be observed *because* they are contained in the former, not the latter. For example, the basic obligation for man to worship his Creator is something all people of every place and time can know simply by reason. It is part of the natural law written on the human heart (Rom. 2:14–15a). The Ten Commandments are often cited as examples of the natural law. Christians are obliged to follow them not because they are cited in the Old Testament law, but because they are part of the natural law. For example, we can know by reason alone that certain actions are immoral—to kill the innocent, to take what does not belong to us, to cheat on our spouses, etc.

Regarding Sabbath worship, we can know by reason alone that we are obliged to worship our Creator. But we cannot know in the same way that worship should take place *on Saturday* (the Sabbath) every week. That part of the Sabbath worship commandment is not part of the natural law at all, but was simply a law imposed upon the Jews for the discipline of their nation.

Other people had the authority to choose for themselves the time they set aside for worship. For Christians now, it makes sense to do this on Sunday. The *Catechism* explains, "The celebration of Sunday observes the moral commandment inscribed by nature in the human heart to render to God an outward, visible, public, and regular worship as a sign of his universal beneficence to all. Sunday worship fulfills the moral command of the Old Covenant, taking up its rhythm and spirit in the weekly celebration of the Creator and Redeemer of his people" (CCC 2176). In other words, Old Testament law required, as a discipline, that the Jews worship on Saturday. Similarly, the Church obliges Catholics to worship on Sunday, the day of the Lord's resurrection.

Like the majority of the law found in the Ten Commandments, the Church's teaching on the immorality of homosexual activity is part of the natural law. People of every time and place can know this through reason alone and are bound by it even without explicit teaching on it. It wasn't absolutely necessary for God to include such teaching in Old Testament law, nor was it absolutely necessary to include it in the New Testament (even though both contain ample teaching in this regard—see Answer 2).

In summary, Christians are bound to the law of Christ, which includes the natural law. Old Testament law contains elements of natural law—e.g., the condemnation of homosexual activity—to which Christians are bound for *that* reason, not because of their inclusion in the Old Testament. Christians do not have liberty on such issues. But Christians are not and have never been bound by Old Testament law for its own sake, and those elements of Old Testament law that are not part of the natural law—e.g., regarding pork and the obligation to worship *on Saturday*—were only ever binding on the Israelites. Christians are to follow the Church, not the Old Testament, on those issues.

6. Wasn't Jesus' apparent silence about homosexuality his tacit approval of it?

Attempting to win Christians over to their side, advocates wishing to normalize homosexual activity often assert that Jesus would approve of their agenda. They ground their assertion in the claim that Jesus never said anything at all about homosexuality. Not once do the Gospels record him explicitly condemning homosexual acts as sinful. Therefore, they say, Jesus would approve of homosexual acts and even same-sex "marriage," so Christians should be supportive of these as well.

Although it is true that the Gospels do not record Jesus explicitly condemning homosexual acts, they do record his implicit condemnation. Jesus taught that marriage is between a man and a woman, as it was instituted by God with Adam and Eve. Genesis 2:24 states, "Therefore a man leaves his father and his mother and cleaves to his wife, and they become one flesh." According to Matthew, Jesus reaffirms this:

> Have you not read that he who made them from the beginning made them male and female, and said, "For this reason a man shall leave his father and mother and be joined to his wife, and the two shall become one flesh"? So, they are no longer two but one flesh. What therefore God has joined together, let not man put asunder (Matt. 19:4–6).

Even so, activists insist that if Jesus truly condemned homosexual activity, he would have taught explicitly about it. His silence on the matter, the claim goes, is deafening. But to conclude on his apparent silence about them alone that he in any way approved of homosexual acts is faulty reasoning. It commits a logical fallacy known as *argumentum ex silentio* (Latin for "argument from silence"). According to this faulty reasoning, Jesus is not on record against it, so he must be for it. Such an argument bases its conclusion on a supposed lack of evidence to the contrary rather than on the existence of any evidence one way or the other. In reality, lack of evidence does not prove anything.

The truth is, the fact that the Gospels do not contain a record of Jesus doing something does not mean that he did not do it. It could be that the Gospel writers chose not to record it for one reason or another. For example, their intended audiences might already have firmly grasped the immorality of homosexual acts. Whatever the reason, the Gospels simply do not contain an exhaustive record of all of Jesus' teaching. John tells us as much at the end of his Gospel: "But there are also many other things which Jesus did; were every one of them to be written, I suppose that the world itself could not contain the books that would be written" (John 21:25). The *Catechism* addresses this as well: "Many things about Jesus of interest to human curiosity do not figure in the Gospels. Almost nothing is said about his hidden life at Nazareth, and even a great part of his public life is not recounted" (CCC 514).

So it could be that Jesus *did* explicitly condemn homosexual acts in his public ministry on earth, but his condemnations were not recorded in the Gospels. In fact, it is reasonable to assert that he did do so, because homosexual acts were condemned in the Old Testament before Jesus as well as in the New Testament after him (see Answer 2).

In the New Testament, it is primarily in Paul's writings that homosexual acts are explicitly condemned. In his letter to the Galatians, Paul reminds us of where he received his teaching: "For I would have you know, brethren, that the gospel which was preached by me is not man's gospel. For I did not receive it from man, nor was I taught it, but it came through a revelation of Jesus Christ" (Gal. 1:11–13).

Paul was the last apostle to be sent by Jesus (1 Cor. 15:8), and we should expect that he received the same assurances that Jesus provided to the other apostles. Jesus promised his apostles that the Holy Spirit would (among other things) "bring to your remembrance all that I have said to you" (John 14:26). Paul certainly shared in this assurance.

Additionally, when Jesus sent out representatives, he told them, "He who hears you hears me, and he who rejects you rejects me, and he who rejects me rejects him who sent me" (Luke 10:16). Thus, since Paul was sent by Jesus, when we "hear" Paul in his writings, we also hear Jesus and his Father. There really is no doubt that Jesus condemned homosexual acts as sinful, so do not be fooled by the faulty reasoning of activists.

7. Was St. Paul just a bigot when it came to homosexuality?

Activists sometimes claim that, for the bulk of Church

history, homosexual acts were not condemned. In fact, the term *homosexual* did not even exist until the nineteenth century, so Church condemnation of such acts is only that recent. They claim that although Paul's writings do condemn activity that today is considered homosexual, he stood alone as a bigot in this regard.

They attempt to dismiss much of Paul's teaching, adding to their own ire by also painting him as a misogynist who believed that women are inferior to men. To fuel their claims, they cite Scripture passages such as 1 Corinthians 14:33–35:

> As in all the churches of the saints, the women should keep silence in the churches. For they are not permitted to speak, but should be subordinate, as even the Law says. If there is anything they desire to know, let them ask their husbands at home. For it is shameful for a woman to speak in church.

Activists claim that Paul's misogynistic teaching was not repeated by others, and it clearly fell out of favor as Jesus' broad message of equality prevailed. Similarly, they claim, Paul's homosexual bigotry fell away, only to be revived by the modern Church. Historical Christianity, they say, simply did not condemn homosexual acts.

It is true that Paul's instructions concerning women in churches were later revised, but what activists fail to recognize in this is a distinction between *doctrine* and *discipline*. When discussing much of the New Testament, understanding the difference between the two is crucial.

A discipline is an instruction or a law instituted under the authority of the Church. It is man-made and can be revised, revoked, or even reversed as often as the Church desires. This is not to say that the authority to enact discipline is man-made. Scripture itself records the Church's God-given authority to enact discipline: "whatever you bind on earth shall be bound in heaven, and whatever you loose on earth shall be loosed in heaven" (Matt. 18:18; see also Matt. 16:19). Now, this power to bind and to loose extends beyond discipline, but it certainly includes the authority to enact discipline as well. The *Catechism* states,

> The power to "bind and loose" connotes the authority to absolve sins, to pronounce doctrinal judgments, and to make disciplinary decisions in the Church. Jesus entrusted this authority to the Church through the ministry of the apostles and in particular through the ministry of Peter, the only one to whom he specifically entrusted the keys of the kingdom (CCC 553).

Doctrine, on the other hand, is the teaching of the Church on matters of faith and morals. All such teaching—or at least the basis for it—was handed down to the

Church by Jesus and the apostles in the first century. Scripture refers to doctrine as "the faith which was once for all delivered to the saints" (Jude 1:3). Doctrine can develop over time as the Church comes to understand it better, but it cannot be revised in the same way a discipline can. No one—not even the pope—has the authority to revoke or reverse a doctrine.

Scripture itself is not always sufficient to distinguish between authentic Christian doctrine and authoritatively imposed discipline. It is sometimes necessary to look beyond Scripture for an understanding of such passages. Some of Paul's instructions concerning women clearly were disciplinary in nature, intended only for a limited time and place, and they did, indeed, change later in Church history. Were his teachings concerning homosexual acts merely Pauline discipline as well?

First, it was not only Paul in the New Testament who explicitly condemned homosexual acts. Peter and Jude did so as well (see Answer 2). So Paul is not isolated in this arena. Additionally, Church Fathers in every century of the early Church also condemned homosexual acts (using terms such as *pederasty* [homosexual abuse of boys by men], *effeminacy*, and *unseemliness*). Here are just a few examples:

Didache (A.D. 70): "You shall not commit murder, you shall not commit adultery, you shall not commit pederasty (2.2)."

Clement of Alexandria (A.D. 193): "Conversation about deeds of wickedness is appropriately termed filthy [shameful] speaking, as talk about adultery and pederasty and the like (*The Instructor* 6)."

Novatian (250): "Effeminate manners are disapproved (*The Jewish Foods* 3)."

Basil the Great (367): "He who is guilty of unseemliness with males will be under discipline for the same time as adulterers (*Letters* 217:62)."

John Chrysostom (391): "All of these affections [in Rom. 1:26–27] . . . were vile, but chiefly the mad lust after males (*Homilies on Romans* 4)."

Augustine (400): "[T]hose shameful acts against nature, such as were committed in Sodom, ought everywhere and always to be detested and punished (*Confessions* 3:5:15)."

Countless more examples spanning the history of the Church could be cited. Furthermore, the Church's Magisterium (authoritative teaching office; see Answer 8), often citing Paul's words, has consistently taught—as a matter of doctrine—the immorality of homosexual activity. Thus, Paul's condemnation of homosexuality clearly was and still is put forth as a doctrinal, not a merely disciplinary, matter. So don't be fooled by radical claims of activists who attempt to rewrite Christian history. Though terminology has varied over the centuries, it is an undeniable fact that the Church has *always* condemned homosexual acts.

8. Why should I believe the Catholic Church's Bible interpretations and teachings on homosexuality instead of anyone else's?

When discussing the Bible, Catholics often find themselves at odds with the Scripture interpretations of others. The truth is, correct interpretation of Scripture has always been a serious matter. Even during the Apostolic Age, there was concern about misguided interpretations. Peter wrote, "There are some things in them [Paul's letters] hard to understand, which the ignorant and unstable twist to their own destruction, as they do the other scriptures" (2 Pet. 3:16). He went on to warn Christians, "You therefore, beloved, knowing this beforehand, beware lest you be carried away with the error of lawless men and lose your own stability" (2 Pet. 3:17).

How were early Christians to know who was teaching the truth? Was there a way to discern who was teaching Christ's truth and who was not? There was. Jesus gave certain followers the authority to teach. The early Christians knew they could trust Peter's teaching because he was one of Jesus' apostles. The word *apostle* comes from the Greek word *apostolos*, which denotes one who is sent as a messenger. Early Christians recognized that the apostles were sent by Christ and endowed with the authority to teach in his name.

At the Last Supper, Jesus promised the apostles that the Father "will give you another Counselor, to be with you forever . . . the Holy Spirit, whom the Father will send in my name, he will teach you all things, and bring to your remembrance all that I have said to you. . . . He will guide you into all the truth" (John 14:16, 26; 16:13).

Before his ascension, Jesus instructed the apostles, "Go therefore and make disciples of all nations, baptizing them in the name of the Father and of the Son and of the Holy Spirit, teaching them to observe all that I have commanded you; and lo, I am with you always, to the close of the age" (Matt. 28:19–20).

So the apostles had authority to teach, and they warned Christians to follow only their authentic teachings and Scripture interpretations and to beware those who taught otherwise.

But what happened after they were gone? Scripture indicates that the apostles endowed bishops and elders with their same special teaching authority. For example, in his first letter to Timothy, a bishop, Paul instructs, "Till I come, attend to the public reading of Scripture, to preaching, to teaching. Do not neglect the gift you have, which was given you by prophetic utterance when the council of elders laid their hands upon you" (1 Tim. 4:13–14). Catholics can recognize in this passage Timothy's ordination. Indeed, it is through the sacrament of holy orders that the teaching ministry of the Church is passed on.

The *Catechism* explains,

> No one can give himself the mandate and the mission to proclaim the gospel. . . . No one can bestow grace on himself; it must be given and offered. This fact presupposes ministers of grace, authorized and empowered by Christ. From him, bishops and priests receive the mission and faculty ("the sacred power") to act *in persona Christi Capitis*; deacons receive the strength to serve the people of God in the *diaconia* of liturgy, word, and charity, in communion with the bishop and his presbyterate. The ministry in which Christ's emissaries do and give by God's grace what they cannot do and give by their own powers is called a "sacrament" by the Church's tradition. Indeed, the ministry of the Church is conferred by a special sacrament (CCC 875).

Therefore, not all teachers or Bible scholars are worthy of our confidence. Only the successors of the apostles, through the sacrament of holy orders, can be counted on in their teaching authority and interpretation of Scripture. The Church Fathers were mostly bishops, and every pope's predecessors can be traced back to Peter.

Quoting the Second Vatican Council, the *Catechism* speaks to the importance of apostolic authority in Catholic teaching:

> The task of giving an authentic interpretation of the word of God, whether in its written form or in the form of Tradition, has been entrusted to the living teaching office of the Church alone. Its authority in this matter is exercised in the name of Jesus Christ. This means that the task of interpretation has been entrusted to the bishops in communion with the successor of Peter, the bishop of Rome (CCC 85; *Dei Verbum* 10).

Trusting in this authority, we can be certain that the Catholic Church's authentic Bible interpretations on homosexuality are the correct ones. They come down to us through teachers with God-given authority. We can and should dismiss misguided Scripture interpretations that are contrary to the truth that Jesus wanted all of us to know.

9. How can the Church teach that homosexuality is a sin if God made people that way?

The Catholic Church does not claim to know, from a medical or scientific perspective, precisely what causes same-sex attractions. This is a matter for doctors and scientists to consider. Accordingly, the *Catechism* admits, "[Homosexuality's] psychological genesis remains largely unexplained" (CCC 2357).

Some people broadly assert that, regardless of what Scripture and the Church say, people with homosexual desires seem to be created that way, so God must have intended for their desires to be fulfilled. They claim that sexual inclination is not a human choice, so homosexual behavior is natural for anyone so inclined. Activists go so far as to claim that a homosexual inclination is part of a person's genetic makeup, so it must be morally acceptable for him to engage in homosexual activity to fulfill his biological, God-given desires.

The fact that an attraction is not chosen by a person does not necessarily mean that God chose it for him or that there is a genetic component to it. Human nature has been injured by sin. This has been the case since the fall of Adam and Eve. Baptism saves us from the eternal consequences of original sin, but other injuries still affect our human nature. The *Catechism* explains, "Certain temporal consequences of sin remain in the baptized, such as suffering, illness, death, and such frailties inherent in life as weaknesses of character, and so on, as well as an inclination to sin that Tradition calls *concupiscence*, or metaphorically, 'the tinder for sin' *(fomes peccati)*" (CCC 1264). So it is not God who chooses a person's sinful desires creating him that way. Rather, a person's inclination toward sin is a direct result of sin itself.

Scientific studies of identical twins suggest that same-sex attraction is not genetic at all. The Catholic Medical Association, in *Homosexuality and Hope* (HH) notes,

> If same-sex attraction were genetically determined, then one would expect identical twins to be identical in their sexual attractions. There are, however, numerous reports of identical twins who are not identical in their sexual attractions. . . . Case histories frequently reveal environmental factors which account for the development of different sexual attraction patterns in genetically identical children, supporting the theory that same-sex attraction is a product of the interplay of a variety of environmental factors (I:1).

Many scientists believe that if it ever is determined that there is some genetic component to same-sex attraction, at most, it might be something that, as with other genes tied to behavior, predisposes a person to the inclination, making him more susceptible to it but not determining it.

Environmental factors act on a predisposition, arousing it in the person who possesses it. For example, some studies have suggested a correlation between a detached father-son relationship and the prevalence of same-sex attractions. This is something that can be avoided. The Catholic Medical Association states, "If the emotional and developmental needs of each child are properly met by both family and peers, the development of same-sex attraction is very unlikely" (HH 3). (This is not to place blame on anyone. Same-sex attraction is a complex disorder.)

With environmental factors playing a role in a susceptible person's life, his own entertaining the inclination to homosexual acts may cause it to begin to feel natural for him. In other words, the more he indulges in homosexual thoughts and actions, the more normal they seem in his own mind. This can happen with any sinful desire, but it doesn't change the fact that the action itself remains sinful. The *Catechism* explains, "Sin creates a proclivity to sin; it engenders vice by repetition of the same acts. This results in perverse inclinations which cloud conscience and corrupt the concrete judgment of good and evil. Thus, sin tends to reproduce itself and reinforce itself, but it cannot destroy the moral sense at its root" (CCC 1865).

Regardless of the cause of the attraction, Scripture has revealed and the Church has always taught that homosexual activity is never moral. The attraction itself is quite irrelevant to the immorality of the act. Indeed, most, if not all, sins contain a component of attraction. For example, no one chooses to be an alcoholic. Certainly, some people are inclined to drink too much, but this does not excuse the immorality of drunkenness. Alcoholism is not a morally acceptable alternative lifestyle.

The same holds true for disordered sexual desires. Indeed, some people are sexually attracted to children, but reasonable people agree that such an inclination cannot be morally acted upon. Likewise, zoophiles should not engage in sexual activity with animals, kleptomaniacs should not steal, and serial killers should not murder. The sobering fact is that our fallen human nature leads to disordered desires and sinful inclinations, but the presence of an attraction or inclination does not make that attraction or inclination normal or morally acceptable to act on.

10. Is Church teaching on homosexuality tantamount to slavery?

People who disagree with Catholic teaching about homosexuality sometimes attempt to equate the Church's doctrine with the imposition of slavery: persons with same-sex attractions are not *free* to be themselves. Activists attempt to align their plight with that of slaves in nineteenth-century America. In reality, their arguments reveal a fundamental misunderstanding about the true nature of freedom. We could simply dismiss their arguments on the basis that race and homosexual behavior cannot be compared: the former concerns demographics, whereas the latter involves chosen acts. But interestingly, New Testament sacred writers sometimes used slavery as an analogy when discussing moral issues. They came to a quite different conclusion from where the activists end up about who is truly enslaved.

St. Paul presents a slavery analogy in his epistle to the Romans:

> Do you not know that if you yield yourselves to any one as obedient slaves, you are slaves of the one whom you obey, either of sin, which leads to death, or of obedience, which leads to righteousness? But thanks be to God, that you who were once slaves of sin have become obedient from the heart to the standard of teaching to which you were committed, and, having been set free from sin, have become slaves of righteousness (Rom. 6:16–18).

In this first analogy, everyone is considered a slave (or "servant"; Greek, *doulos*) either to sin or to righteousness, but sin leads to death (hell), whereas righteousness leads to sanctification and eternal life (heaven). In essence, the two propositions are quite opposite, sin being more analogous to slavery and righteousness to freedom. In his second epistle, St. Peter concurs with Paul as he warns of false prophets and teachers: "uttering loud boasts of folly, they entice with licentious passions of the flesh. . . . They promise them freedom, but they themselves are slaves of corruption; for whatever overcomes a man, to that he is enslaved" (2 Pet. 2:18–19).

Paul often referred to himself as a slave of God (e.g., see Rom. 1:1; Gal. 1:10), which is a good thing, but he warned against slavery to sin (e.g., see Titus 2:3; 3:1, 3). Ultimately, Paul does recognize obedience to righteousness to be *freedom* and obedience to sin to be *slavery*: "do not submit again to a yoke of slavery. . . . For you were called to freedom, brethren; only do not use your freedom as an opportunity for the flesh [i.e., sin]" (Gal. 5:1, 13).

Paul explains here that following Christ leads to true freedom. We do this with the help of the Holy Spirit: "now the Lord is the Spirit, and where the Spirit of the Lord is, there is freedom" (2 Cor. 3:17). Peter, again, concurs: "live as free men, yet without using your freedom as a pretext for evil; but live as servants [or slaves] of God" (1 Pet. 2:16).

So, according to Paul and Peter, true freedom does not mean that a person does whatever he feels like or is tempted or inclined to do. That's not really freedom at all; instead, often, it is slavery to sin. The *Catechism* explains,

> The exercise of freedom does not imply a right to say or do everything. It is false to maintain that man, the subject of this freedom, is an individual who is fully self-sufficient and whose finality is the satisfaction of his own interests in the enjoyment of earthly goods. . . . By deviating from the moral law, man violates his own freedom, becomes imprisoned

within himself, disrupts neighborly fellowship, and rebels against divine truth (CCC 1740).

The solution to such a predicament and the way to true freedom are found in Jesus' own words:

Jesus then said to the Jews who had believed in him, "If you continue in my word, you are truly my disciples, and you will know the truth, and the truth will make you free." They answered him, "We are descendants of Abraham, and have never been in bondage to anyone. How is it that you say, 'You will be made free'?" Jesus answered them, "Truly, truly, I say to you, everyone who commits sin is a slave to sin. The slave does not continue in the house forever; the son continues forever. So, if the Son makes you free, you will be free indeed" (John 8:31–36).

Thus, embracing the truth (however difficult), making it active in our lives, and rejecting the inclination to sin are what true freedom is all about. On the other hand, embracing our sinful desires and embellishing such lifestyles make for true slavery. The *Catechism* explains, "The more one does what is good, the freer one becomes. There is no true freedom except in the service of what is good and just. The choice to disobey and do evil is an abuse of freedom and leads to the slavery of sin" (CCC 1733).

Considering all this, the one who is truly enslaved is the person with same-sex attractions who rejects the truth in favor of his own desires, not the person who resists his inclination to sin in favor of acting according to the truth that sets him free.

11. Is Church teaching on homosexuality judgmental?

When Catholics express the truth about homosexuality to others, they are often accused of being "judgmental" and are promptly informed that the Bible teaches us not to judge others. Nowadays, opponents are also likely to quote Pope Francis, who once said, "If a person is gay and seeks God and has good will, who am I to judge?" (More on this later.)

Does the Bible really teach that we are never to judge? When pressed to show where Scripture supports their claim, most people quote Jesus' words found in the Gospel of Matthew: "judge not, that you not be judged" (Matt. 7:1). They usually stop there, with the clear conviction that this verse proves that the Bible teaches that we are not to pass any form of judgment on others.

A closer look at this verse and other related verses uncovers a different understanding of Jesus' teaching. Here is the full context of Jesus' words:

Judge not, that you be not judged. For with the judgment you pronounce you will be judged, and the measure you give will be the measure you get. Why do you see the speck that is in your brother's eye, but do not notice the log that is in your own eye? Or how can you say to your brother, "Let me take the speck out of your eye," when there is the log in your own eye? You hypocrite, first take the log out of your own eye, and then you will see clearly to take the speck out of your brother's eye (Matt. 7:1–5).

If we break this passage down line by line, it becomes clear that Jesus is not telling his disciples they should never judge the behavior of others. Rather, he is cautioning them to live righteous lives themselves so their judgment of others' behavior will not be *rash* judgment and their efforts will be effective in admonishing their neighbors.

"Judge not, that you be not judged." By itself, this statement could be construed to mean that one may escape even God's judgment simply by not judging the behavior of others. But everyone is judged by God, so this cannot be a proper understanding. Jesus goes on to reformulate his statement in a positive way: "with the judgment you pronounce you will be judged, and the measure you give will be the measure you get." Jesus indeed expects his disciples to judge, but he warns that they will be judged in a like manner.

In the next two lines, Jesus cautions against hypocrisy: "Why do you see the speck that is in your brother's eye, but do not notice the log that is in your own eye? Or how can you say to your brother, 'Let me take the speck out of your eye,' when there is the log in your own eye?" Judging hypocritically is not effective.

Jesus then explains how to judge rightly: "First take the log out of your own eye, and then you will see clearly to take the speck out of your brother's eye." There can be no doubt that those final words—"take the speck out of your brother's eye"—are, indeed, permission—a commandment, even—to judge so long as it is done rightly.

Other Bible passages, some of which on the surface indicate a condemnation of judging others' behavior, may be treated similarly in their full context. In fact, the exhortation to rightly judge the behavior of others can be found throughout the Bible. (For example, see Lev. 19:15; Matt. 18:15–17; John 7:24; 1 Cor. 5:12–13; 1 Cor. 6:2–18.) The Catholic Church teaches likewise but cautions, as Jesus did, against rash judgment:

> To avoid rash judgment, everyone should be careful to interpret insofar as possible his neighbor's thoughts, words, and deeds in a favorable way: every good Christian ought to be more ready to give a favorable interpretation to another's statement than to condemn it. But if he cannot do so, let him ask how the other understands it. And if the latter understands it badly, let the former correct him with love. If that does not suffice, let the Christian try all suitable ways

to bring the other to a correct interpretation so that he may be saved (CCC 2477–2478).

Having said all this, there is a big difference between judging another's *behavior* and judging *the eternal state of his soul*. The latter judgment belongs only to God (John 5:22–30). This is the type of judgment about which Pope Francis spoke.

So, when faced with the immoral behavior of loved ones, how can Catholics be sure to rightly judge behavior? In Jesus' own words, we must start by taking the logs out of our own eyes—by making sure we are doing the best we can to live a life of good example. We must also strive to form our consciences correctly so that we know sin when we see it. Finally, we should be careful not to jump to conclusions about another's culpability in sin. Doing all this will help to ensure that "judgmental" admonitions are seen as the loving actions they are intended to be—meant to help others live their lives in ways that are pleasing to God. Only then can our efforts be effective in helping to take these ugly specks out of our brothers' eyes.

12. Is Church teaching on homosexuality intolerant?

Possibly the longest held maxim of homosexual activists is that of "tolerance." Since Catholics believe that homosexual activity is always immoral, we have long been considered an intolerant bunch. Some activist organizations exist for the sole purpose of promoting Christian tolerance—specifically tolerance of homosexual activity. But the form of tolerance they promote equates with approval and support of sinful behavior. Anything less than their ever further reaching goal is viewed as condemnation and labeled "intolerance." To promote their agenda, such groups frequently cite the Gospel story of the woman caught in adultery, in which Jesus prevents the sinner's stoning and sends her away without condemnation (John 8:3–11). Jesus' actions are said to be supportive—in a word, tolerant.

Indeed, Jesus said to the adulteress, "Has no one condemned you? . . . Neither do I condemn you (John 8:11)." But this doesn't mean he supported her sinful behavior or expected her accusers to do so. In fact, he admonished the adulteress, "Do not sin again (John 8:11)." If this episode provides an example for Christian behavior, it is this: do not condemn (see Answer 11), but also do not condone sinful behavior. This is precisely the teaching of the Catholic Church concerning the treatment of people experiencing same-sex attractions. The *Catechism* exhorts non-condemnation *as well as* rejection of the sinful behavior (CCC 2357–2358; see Answer 2). So Catholic teaching is consistent with Jesus' example and certainly does not support a definition of tolerance that condones or supports immoral behavior.

What do other biblical passages say about Christian tolerance?

Most English translations of the New Testament today do not include the word "tolerance" at all. The closest many come is a few instances of the word "tolerable" (Greek, *anektoteron*), but that word is not used in the context of Christian behavior (see Matt. 10:5–15; Matt. 11:20–24; Luke 10:1–14). The Revised Standard Version, a relatively literal translation, contains only one other instance of any form of the word *tolerance* at all: "But I have this against you, that you tolerate the woman Jezebel, who calls herself a prophetess and is teaching and beguiling my servants to practice immorality and to eat food sacrificed to idols" (Rev. 2:20). Here, Christ actually *rejects* tolerance—he rebukes the church in Thyatira for its tolerance of Jezebel, who, among other things, was influencing Christians to practice immorality. A modern-day attitude that condones or supports homosexual behavior could be rejected on this basis alone. But there is more.

Although use of the word "tolerance" is scant in the New Testament, there are ample other biblical examples of what Christian tolerance should look like. Tolerating undesirable behavior extends only to the point of putting up with it, enduring it, bearing it for a greater good. It never crosses the line into condoning or supporting immorality. For example, on dealing with obstinate disbelief, Jesus says, "O faithless generation, how long am I to be with you? How long am I to bear with you?" (Mark 9:19). Similarly, Paul exhorts "forbearing one another" and "enduring" persecution (see 1 Cor. 4:12; Eph. 4:1; Col. 3:12). These passages indicate that there are times when we must put up with the undesirable actions of others without condemning them (see Answer 11), but they do *not* indicate that we are to condone or support sinful behavior.

Finally, there is even a point at which Christian tolerance means distancing ourselves from obstinate sinners to protect ourselves and our loved ones from them. This approach seems most evident in the following teaching of Jesus: "If your brother sins against you, go and tell him his fault, between you and him alone. If he listens to you, you have gained your brother. But if he does not listen, take one or two others along with you, that every word may be confirmed by the evidence of two or three witnesses. If he refuses to listen to them, tell it to the church; and if he refuses to listen even to the church, let him be to you as a Gentile and a tax collector" (Matt. 18:15–17). Paul teaches similarly, "Now we command you, brethren, in the name of our Lord Jesus Christ, that you keep away from any brother who is living in idleness and not in accord with the tradition that you received from us" (2 Thess. 3:6).

Ultimately, rejecting a person's sinful behavior without condemnation can lead that person to repentance and salvation. Paul indicates this in God's own example: "do you presume upon the riches of [God's] kindness and forbearance and patience? Do you not know that God's kindness is meant to lead you to repentance?" (Rom. 2:4) That's the goal of authentic Christian tolerance: reconciliation with God and, ultimately, salvation of the sinner.

13. Is Church teaching on homosexuality not truly loving, but hateful?

Because we do not condone homosexual behavior, Catholics are often accused of being hateful. Homosexual behavior is said by activists to be a loving act between two same-sex persons who love each other. To reject the sexual expression of their "love" is to be hateful toward them. Of course, Catholics recognize that same-sex sexual activity is always immoral (see Answer 2) and, so, is not truly loving at all. Not condoning immersion into sinful behavior is the truly loving act. Ironically, our love ends up being called hate.

English-speakers use the word *love* in many ways. Not all "love" is the same. The word has broad meaning in our language. Such is not the case with every language, especially in terms of the love of other people. Pope Benedict XVI points this out in his encyclical *Deus Caritas Est* (DCE):

> That love between man and woman which is neither planned nor willed, but somehow imposes itself upon human beings, was called *eros* by the ancient Greeks. Let us note straight away that the

Greek Old Testament uses the word *eros* only twice, while the New Testament does not use it at all: of the three Greek words for love, *eros*, *philia* (the love of friendship), and *agape*, New Testament writers prefer the last, which occurs rather infrequently in Greek usage. . . . The tendency to avoid the word *eros*, together with the new vision of love expressed through the word *agape*, clearly points to something new and distinct about the Christian understanding of love (DCE 3).

So there are at least three types of love people can share with one another. Certainly, there is some overlap among them, but Christians are especially called always to express a certain type of love above all others.

When asked what was the greatest commandment, Jesus answered, "You shall love the Lord your God with all your heart, and with all your soul, and with all your mind. This is the great and first commandment. And a second is like it, you shall love your neighbor as yourself" (Matt. 22:36–39). It is the second commandment mentioned here that Christians must be concerned with when dealing with our fellow man. The word translated as "love" comes from the Greek word *agape*, the word cited by Pope Benedict as the one preferred by New Testament writers, expressing "something new and distinct about the Christian understanding of love."

If *eros* and *philia* are concerned primarily with our relationships with others, *agape* is concerned primarily with our own relationships with God—as well as with *each other's* relationships with God. Christian love should be shared with everyone, regardless of our feelings. It is the kind of love that Jesus commanded we show even to those we do not like: "Love your enemies" (Luke 6:27).

To express Christian love, we must first know which behaviors are pleasing to God and which are not, and then we must share that knowledge with others for everyone's good. Paul expressed this when he wrote, "Let love be genuine; hate what is evil, hold fast to what is good" (Rom. 12:9).

Pope Benedict wrote about this in his encyclical *Caritas in Veritate* (CV), in which he referred to Christian love more precisely as *charity*: "to defend the truth, to articulate it with humility and conviction, and to bear witness to it in life are therefore exacting and indispensable forms of charity. . . . To love someone is to desire that person's good and to take effective steps to secure it" (CV 1, 7).

To do less than this is to fail to fully love as Christ expects us to. Yet less is what activists expect—a shallow "anything goes" form of coddling that does not have the other's salvation in mind. Christian truth is not important, and the highest form of love comes to be seen as hatred. There is no more room for Christ.

Benedict XVI explains,

Without truth, charity degenerates into sentimentality. Love becomes an empty shell, to be filled in an arbitrary way. In a culture without truth, this is the fatal risk facing love. It falls prey to contingent subjective emotions and opinions, the word "love" is abused and distorted, to the point where it comes to mean the opposite. . . .

A Christianity of charity without truth would be more or less interchangeable with a pool of good sentiments, helpful for social cohesion, but of little relevance. In other words, there would no longer be any real place for God in the world (CV 3–4).

Thus, authentic Christian love is rejected; it is seen not as love at all, but as hate. Christians are therefore persecuted and hated in return. But take consolation: Jesus knew that this would happen, yet he commanded the *agape* form of love anyway: "this I command you, to love one another. If the world hates you, know that it has hated me before it hated you. . . . Remember the word that I said to you, 'A servant is not greater than his master.' If they persecuted me, they will persecute you" (John 15:17–18, 20).

14. What does the Church teach about "same-sex marriage"?

Persons of the same sex are, quite simply, not capable of marrying one another. To understand this, one must first grasp what marriage actually *is*.

The *Catechism* introduces the topic of marriage this way:

> The matrimonial covenant, by which a man and a woman establish between themselves a partnership of the whole of life, is by its nature ordered toward the good of the spouses and the procreation and education of offspring; this covenant between baptized persons has been raised by Christ the Lord to the dignity of a sacrament (CCC 1601, emphasis added).

Notice that marriage is a covenantal partnership between *a man and a woman*. By definition, this is so. Indeed, the term "marriage" identifies this—and only this—specific and unique type of relationship. This is by God's design:

> So, God created man in his own image, in the image of God he created him; male and female he created them. . . . Therefore, a man leaves his father and his mother and cleaves to his wife, and they become one flesh (Gen. 1:27; 2:24).

Why is this? Man and woman are physically designed to sexually unite for procreation. The Church's

Congregation for the Doctrine of the Faith empha-sizes this in its document *Considerations Regarding Proposals to Give Legal Recognition to Unions Between Homosexual Persons* (UHP):

> Men and women are equal as persons and comple-mentary as male and female. Sexuality is something that pertains to the physical-biological realm and has also been raised to a new level—the personal level—where nature and spirit are united. Marriage is instituted by the Creator as a form of life in which a communion of persons is realized involving the use of the sexual faculty (3).

It should be obvious to any reasonable person that humans are created "male and female" so that the two sexes may engage in procreative activity. This sexual complementarity of the couple leads husband and wife to become parents who care for and raise children to-gether. In other words, they make a family, the foun-dational building block of humanity.

A beautiful aspect of this order is that man and woman are thereby called to work with God in the propagation of the human species! We procreate the bodies, and God creates the souls (CCC 366). Indeed, the Church states, "God has willed to give the union of man and woman a special participation in his work of creation. Thus, he blessed the man and the woman with the words 'Be fruitful and multiply' (Gen. 1:28). Therefore, in the Creator's plan, sexual complementarity and fruitfulness belong to the very nature of marriage" (UHP 3).

One way to emphasize how important true marriage is to God's plan for humanity is to realize the fact that Jesus endowed Christian marriage with sacramental graces. The CDF explains,

> The marital union of man and woman has been elevated by Christ to the dignity of a sacrament. The Church teaches that Christian marriage is an efficacious sign of the covenant between Christ and the Church (Eph. 5:32). This Christian meaning of marriage, far from diminishing the profoundly human value of the marital union between man and woman, confirms and strengthens it (UHP 3).

Considering all this, it is quite easy to see why not just *any* relationship can or should be recognized as marriage. Relationships that are not marriages but attempt to mimic them—such as same-sex relationships—are offensive to the institution of marriage itself and must always be avoided. Pope Francis recently reiterated the Church's constant teaching on this subject in his post-synodal apostolic exhortation *Amoris Laetitia* (AL): "As for proposals to place unions between homosexual persons on the same level as marriage, there are absolutely no grounds for considering homosexual unions to be in any way similar or even remotely analogous to God's plan for marriage and family" (AL 251).

As a final note on this topic, it should be pointed out that the Church does not have the power or authority to change all this—nor does secular society: "The Church can never be so callous. It is true that her clear position cannot be revised by pressure from civil legislation or the trend of the moment" (UHP 9).

Even in places where the legal definition of the word "marriage" has been expanded to include same-sex relationships, those relationships are not truly marriages. The Church says it this way:

> No ideology can erase from the human spirit the certainty that marriage exists solely between a man and a woman, who by mutual personal gift, proper and exclusive to themselves, tend toward the communion of their persons. In this way, they mutually perfect each other, in order to cooperate with God in the procreation and upbringing of new human lives (UHP 2).

Therefore, Christians should always keep in mind God's plan for marriage and never give in to societal pressures that seek to erase or redefine what God has so eloquently instituted for the good of humanity. (For more on what marriage is and is not, see *20 Answers: Divorce & Remarriage*.)

15. Why does the Church teach that sterile oppo site-sex couples are able to marry, but same-sex couples are not?

As stated in the previous answer, the *Catechism* introduces the topic of marriage this way:

> The matrimonial covenant, by which a man and a woman establish between themselves a partnership of the whole of life, is by its nature ordered toward the good of the spouses and the procreation and education of offspring; this covenant between baptized persons has been raised by Christ the Lord to the dignity of a sacrament (CCC 1601, emphasis added).

Notice this time that marriage is said to be "ordered toward" certain things, including the procreation of offspring. This means that marriage must always involve a man and a woman, because only sexual activity between two such human beings is ordered toward procreation. Simply put, it takes a man and a woman to make a baby. Whatever the relationship might be between a man and another man or between a woman and another woman, it cannot ever make a baby and, therefore, cannot ever be marriage. Such a combination of human beings does not include the anatomy necessary to produce a child.

Frankly, having children is one of the ends of marriage that homosexual relationships are not equipped to share. The Congregation for the Doctrine of the Faith's *Declaration on Certain Questions Concerning Sexual Ethics* (*Persona Humana* or PH) states, "For according to the objective moral order, homosexual relations are acts which lack an essential and indispensable finality" (PH VIII). That finality is their ordering toward procreation.

The CDF's document *Considerations Regarding Proposals to Give Legal Recognition to Unions Between Homosexual Persons* explains, "Homosexual acts close the sexual act to the gift of life. They do not proceed from a genuine affective and sexual complementarity" (UHP 4). As such, homosexual acts are essentially selfish acts.

The CDF's *Letter to the Bishops of the Catholic Church on the Pastoral Care of Homosexual Persons* further explains,

> To choose someone of the same sex for one's sexual activity is to annul the rich symbolism and meaning, not to mention the goals, of the Creator's sexual design. Homosexual activity is not a complementary union, able to transmit life; and so it thwarts the call to a life of that form of self-giving which the gospel says is the essence of Christian living. This does not mean that homosexual persons are not often generous and giving of themselves; but when

they engage in homosexual activity they confirm within themselves a disordered sexual inclination which is essentially self-indulgent (CHP 7).

So what about sterility in opposite-sex couples? How are their sexual acts at all different from homosexual acts? Sterility—the inability to procreate—does not impede marriage for heterosexual couples because their sexual activity remains *ordered toward procreation* even though it does not result in pregnancy. What is required for marriage is the ability to complete the marital act, not the ability to have children. Thus, sterility itself is not an impediment to marriage.

The *Catechism of the Catholic Church* phrases it this way: sex acts must be "ordered *per se* to the procreation of human life" (CCC 2366). Sterility does not change the fact that the act itself is ordered toward procreation.

Humanae Vitae (HV) explains,

The sexual activity, in which husband and wife are intimately and chastely united with one another, through which human life is transmitted, is, as the recent council recalled, "noble and worthy." It does not, moreover, cease to be legitimate even when, for reasons independent of their will, it is foreseen to be infertile. For its natural adaptation to the expression and strengthening of the union of husband and wife is not thereby suppressed. The fact is, as experience shows, that new life is not the result of each and every act of sexual intercourse. God has wisely ordered laws of nature and the incidence of fertility in such a way that successive births are already naturally spaced through the inherent operation of these laws. The Church, nevertheless, in urging men to the observance of the precepts of the natural law, which it interprets by its constant doctrine, teaches that each and every marital act must of necessity retain its intrinsic relationship to the procreation of human life (HV 11).

It should be noted here that, although sterility does not impede marriage, the permanent inability, prior to the wedding, to engage in the sexual act (for example, due to impotence) *is* an impediment.

Finally, questions often arise about other methods of having babies. Science and medicine have revealed ways in which couples can procreate without the sexual act. Can't these methods allow same-sex couples to procreate and so get married? The bottom-line answer is no, in part because such methods of procreation are immoral—for everyone, even opposite-sex couples.

The *Catechism* makes this clear:

Techniques that entail the dissociation of husband and wife, by the intrusion of a person other than the couple (donation of sperm or ovum, surrogate uterus), are gravely immoral. These techniques (heterologous artificial insemination and fertilization) infringe the child's right to be born of a father and mother known to him and bound to each other by marriage (CCC 2376).

The CDF addresses this issue as it pertains to homosexual acts lacking the procreative aspect of marriage: "The possibility of using recently discovered methods of artificial reproduction, beyond involving a grave lack of respect for human dignity, does nothing to alter this inadequacy" (UHP 7).

16. Should I attend a "gay wedding"?

With civil recognition of same-sex unions as "marriages" in many locations, questions about whether it is legitimate to attend a "gay wedding" have become increasingly common. Relatives, friends, and co-workers—sometimes even Catholic ones—plan such ceremonies and expect others to rejoice in them as they would in a wedding. Some argue, "Gay marriage is legitimate under the eyes of the government—it is the law of the land now—so embrace it and join us in the celebration." What is a serious Catholic to do?

One problem with this line of thinking is that there are other laws to consider in addition to "the law of the land." Indeed, Catholics must always recognize that ecclesiastical law (i.e., Church law) is superior to civil law, and it *does not* recognize same-sex relationships as marriages (see Answer 14). Yet it is common practice today to ignore this fact.

This can be an especially difficult factor to bring up when dealing with dissenting or fallen away Catholics. But imagine an American citizen ignoring a federal law or proclaiming, "I don't consider myself an American anymore, so I don't have to worry about breaking the country's laws." It doesn't work that way! A citizen cannot arbitrarily exempt himself from justly enacted laws. The same applies to state laws. If a man fails to get a marriage license, the state will not recognize his marriage. He might move to another state, but he will then become subject to the laws of that state. Being a citizen of the Catholic Church is somewhat similar, but there is no place where one may move that he is no longer under the jurisdiction of the Catholic Church. The Church has universal jurisdiction.

How can the Catholic Church defend its universal legal authority? *It is God-given authority.* Jesus gave the Church the authority to enact laws that bind its citizens (see Answers 5, 7). Nevertheless, God's law as expressed in ecclesiastical law is often ignored, and Catholics are placed in the difficult position of explaining why they cannot rejoice in same-sex relationships or "gay weddings." Complicating the issue is the fact that the Catholic Church does not explicitly address the question of whether or not to attend such a ceremony. However, the Church does more broadly address words and attitudes that encourage and confirm others in objectively wrong behavior.

The *Catechism* states,

> Every word or attitude is forbidden which by *flattery, adulation, or complaisance* encourages and confirms another in malicious acts and perverse conduct. Adulation is a grave fault if it makes one an accomplice in another's vices or grave sins. Neither the desire to be of service nor friendship justifies duplicitous speech. Adulation is a venial sin when it only seeks to be agreeable, to avoid evil, to meet a need, or to obtain legitimate advantages (CCC 2480).

Additionally, scandal—which is when our actions lead others into sin or error—must be a considered. What would attending the wedding say to the couple and to others? The *Catechism* explains,

> Scandal is an attitude or behavior which leads another to do evil. The person who gives scandal becomes his neighbor's tempter. He damages virtue and integrity; he may even draw his brother into spiritual death. Scandal is a grave offense if by deed or omission another is deliberately led into a grave offense.

Scandal takes on a particular gravity by reason of the authority of those who cause it or the weakness of those who are scandalized. It prompted our Lord to utter this curse: "Whoever causes one of these little ones who believe in me to sin, it would be better for him to have a great millstone fastened round his neck and to be drowned in the depth of the sea." Scandal is grave when given by those who by nature or office are obliged to teach and educate others. Jesus reproaches the scribes and Pharisees on this account: he likens them to wolves in sheep's clothing (CCC 2284–2285).

Therefore, in consideration of all this, I cannot recommend attending *any* ceremony or "wedding" that will not result in a valid marriage according to ecclesiastical law. Instead, I recommend charitably explaining the reasons for declining an invitation as well as expressing hope and offering guidance for the couple in amending their plans. Direction from an orthodox Catholic spiritual director is often a good idea in handling such difficult situations. Spiritual direction can help ensure that one's obligations to family and friends are wisely met without the foolish contravention of God's laws.

17. Is it okay to support legal recognition of same-sex unions without calling them marriages?

In many legal jurisdictions, homosexual advocates have pushed for legal recognition of their relationships even if they do not call them marriages. Often, they advocate for such unions to enjoy the same legal benefits that marriage does, including an allowance for adopting children. Aside from the moral issue (see Answer 2), the truth is that such recognition does violence to the institution of marriage as well as to children and the family in society. Keep in mind that legal recognition of same-sex unions goes beyond mere toleration of homosexual activity (see Answer 12). Formal recognition serves to structure society around illegitimate relationships and give scandal to the ignorant and the young, who should be educated properly on what marriage and family are all about.

Fortunately, the Congregation for the Doctrine of the Faith takes up this matter in great detail in its document *Considerations Regarding Proposals to Give Legal Recognition to Unions Between Homosexual Persons*. In this document, the CDF notes this:

> Homosexual unions are totally lacking in the biological and anthropological elements of marriage and family which would be the basis, on the level of reason, for granting them legal recognition. Such unions are not able to contribute in a proper way to the procreation and survival of the human race (UHP 7).

The CDF goes on to address the problems that arise for marriage, children, and the family when same-sex unions are afforded legal status. We have already touched on issues concerning the institution of marriage itself (see Answer 14), so the violence done to children and the family will be our primary focus here.

First, a child adopted by a same-sex couple is deprived of his right to be conceived in the morally ordered fashion and raised by his biological mother and father. The CDF explains,

As experience has shown, the absence of sexual complementarity in these unions creates obstacles in the normal development of children who would be placed in the care of such persons. They would be deprived of the experience of either fatherhood or motherhood. Allowing children to be adopted by persons living in such unions would actually mean doing violence to these children, in the sense that their condition of dependency would be used to place them in an environment that is not conducive to their full human development. This is gravely immoral and in open contradiction to the principle, recognized also in the United Nations Convention on the Rights of the Child, that the best interests of the child, as the weaker and more vulnerable party, are to be the paramount consideration in every case (UHP 7).

Second, the family's role in the common good of society and the promulgation of the human species is violently diminished when same-sex unions are legally recognized. The definition of marriage—even if not formally redefined—is blurred as well. The CDF explains,

Society owes its continued survival to the family, founded on marriage. The inevitable consequence of legal recognition of homosexual unions would be the redefinition of marriage, which would become, in its legal status, an institution devoid of essential reference to factors linked to heterosexuality: for example, procreation and raising children. If, from the legal standpoint, marriage between a man and a woman were to be considered just one possible form of marriage, the concept of marriage would undergo a radical transformation, with grave detriment to the common good. By putting homosexual unions on a legal plane analogous to that of marriage and the family, the state acts arbitrarily and in contradiction with its duties. . . .

Not even in a remote analogous sense do homosexual unions fulfill the purpose for which marriage and family deserve specific categorical recognition. On the contrary, there are good reasons for holding that such unions are harmful to the proper development of human society, especially if their impact on society were to increase (UHP 8).

For these reasons—the violence done to marriage, children, and the family—society is harmed when same-sex unions are legally equated with marriages, whether they are called marriages or not. Marriage, therefore, deserves protection under the law for the good of everyone. The CDF states,

> Because married couples ensure the succession of generations and are therefore eminently within the public interest, civil law grants them institutional recognition. Homosexual unions, on the other hand, do not need specific attention from the legal standpoint since they do not exercise this function for the common good (UHP 9).

The CDF later concludes,

> The Church teaches that respect for homosexual persons cannot lead in any way to approval of homosexual behavior or to legal recognition of homosexual unions. The common good requires that laws recognize, promote, and protect marriage as the basis of the family, the primary unit of society. Legal recognition of homosexual unions or placing them on the same level as marriage would mean not only the approval of deviant behavior, with the consequence of making it a model in present-day society, but would also obscure basic values which belong to

the common inheritance of humanity. The Church cannot fail to defend these values, for the good of men and women and for the good of society itself (UHP 11).

A final question on this topic often arises: what are citizens to do when legal recognition of same-sex unions has already been granted? The CDF tells us:

Clear and emphatic opposition is a duty. One must refrain from any kind of formal cooperation in the enactment or application of such gravely unjust laws and, as far as possible, from material cooperation on the level of their application. In this area, everyone can exercise the right to conscientious objection (UHP 5).

18. Can homosexuality be cured?

Given the fact that homosexual acts can never be approved under any circumstances (CCC 2357; see also Answer 2), it is natural to hope that there is a cure for the inclination to them. Indeed, the Pontifical Council for the Family hints at such hope: "Especially when the practice of homosexual acts has not become a habit, many cases can benefit from appropriate therapy" (*The Truth and Meaning of Human Sexuality* 104). Even so, much of secular society scoffs at the idea that homosexuality is anything but normal. Catholics are labeled "homophobes," and therapy aimed at treating same-sex attractions has even been legally banned in many areas.

Not all scientists and medical professionals have succumbed to secular pressure. The Catholic Medical Association (CMA), in its publication *Homosexuality and Hope*, asserts that "the labeling of an adolescent, or worse a child, as unchangeably 'homosexual' does the individual a grave disservice. Such adolescents or children can, with appropriate, positive intervention, be given proper guidance to deal with early emotional traumas" (HH I:4).

Although it is true that homosexuality's "psychological genesis remains largely unexplained" (CCC 2357), clinical psychology still seems to be the best hope for treatment. Genetics has not been proven to play a part in homosexuality (see Answer 9), so reputable scientists and medical professionals approach it from a psychological perspective. The CMA sees promise in this: "once convinced that same-sex attraction is not a genetically determined disorder, one is able to hope for prevention and a therapeutic model to greatly mitigate, if not eliminate, same-sex attractions" (HH I:3). Also, "experienced therapists can help individuals uncover and understand the root causes of the emotional trauma which gave rise to their same-sex attractions and then work in therapy to resolve this pain" (HH I:6). Thus, clinical psychologists work with

sufferers of homosexuality, developing therapeutic relationships with them that can lead to varying levels of
relief. The CMA explains,

> Many therapists have written extensively on the
> positive results of therapy for same-sex attraction.
> . . . Reviews of treatment for unwanted same-sex at-
> tractions show that it is as successful as treatment
> for similar psychological problems: about 30% ex-
> perience a freedom from symptoms and another
> 30% experience improvement. . . .
>
> There are also numerous autobiographical re-
> ports from men and women who once believed
> themselves to be unchangeably bound by same-sex
> attractions and behaviors. Many of these men and
> women . . . now describe themselves as free of same-
> sex attraction, fantasy, and behavior. Most of these
> individuals found freedom through participation
> in religion-based support groups, although some
> also had recourse to therapists (HH I:5).

For Christians, successful psychological therapy
may not necessarily mean reversal to a properly ordered sexual inclination or even complete freedom
from same-sex attractions. Rather, the ability to live a
moral life is the key. The CMA explains,

> Some of those who have struggled with same-sex

attractions believe that they are called to a celibate life. They should not be made to feel that they have failed to achieve freedom because they do not experience desires for the other sex. Others wish to marry and have children. There is every reason to hope that many will be able, in time, to achieve this goal. They should not, however, be encouraged to rush into marriage since there is ample evidence that marriage is not a cure for same-sex attractions. With the power of grace, the sacraments, support from the community, and an experienced therapist, a determined individual should be able to achieve the inner freedom promised by Christ (HH I:6).

In other words, chastity should be the primary goal in psychological therapy for homosexuality. This should be no surprise, as chastity is a goal for every Christian, whatever his sexual inclination or state of life might be. The *Catechism* teaches, "Chastity means the successful integration of sexuality within the person and thus the inner unity of man in his bodily and spiritual being" (CCC 2337).

As such, chastity takes various forms. The *Catechism* explains,

People should cultivate [chastity] in the way that is suited to their state of life. Some profess virginity or consecrated celibacy which enables them to give themselves to God alone with an undivided heart in a remarkable manner. Others live in the way prescribed for all by the moral law, whether they are married or single. Married people are called to live conjugal chastity; others practice chastity in continence (CCC 2349).

Thus, for the Christian with same-sex attractions, psychological therapy may be seen as something of a "cure" when it leads to his ability to live a chaste life: "Homosexual persons are called to chastity. By the virtues of self-mastery that teach them inner freedom, at times by the support of disinterested friendship, by prayer and sacramental grace, they can and should gradually and resolutely approach Christian perfection" (CCC 2359).

Recognition of this can provide hope for the same-sex-attracted Christian who desires to live in conformity with Christ and the teachings of his Church.

19. How can I help my loved one who has same-sex attractions?

First, always keep in mind that people with same-sex attractions are children of God, and the Church reminds us that they "must be accepted with respect, compassion, and sensitivity. Every sign of unjust discrimination in their regard should be avoided" (CCC

2358). A simple way to begin putting this into practice today is to be articulate in the language that we use so as not to reduce any person to the disorder from which he suffers. Terms such as "gay man," "lesbian woman," and various other "LGBT" monikers aimed at normalizing same-sex behavior are inherently harmful. The CDF's *Letter to the Bishops of the Catholic Church on the Pastoral Care of Homosexual Persons* explains,

> The human person, made in the image and likeness of God, can hardly be adequately described by a reductionist reference to his or her sexual orientation. . . . Today, the Church provides a badly needed context for the care of the human person when she refuses to consider the person as a "heterosexual" or a "homosexual" and insists that every person has a fundamental identity: the creature of God, and by grace, his child and heir to eternal life (CHP 16).

The Church and individual Catholics still sometimes refer to a person as "a homosexual" or "a homosexual person," but this is a kind of shorthand or negotiated terminology, not an acknowledgment of a homosexual ontology. A more pastoral approach uses terminology such as "a person with same-sex attractions" so as to first recognize his dignity as a person and only then, when necessary, to make reference to the relevant disorder from which he suffers. Recognition of his personhood reminds us that our love for him must put his relationship with God—his salvation—first (see Answer 13).

Second, especially when dealing with Catholics and other Christians, be cautious never to water down the Church's teaching on homosexuality. The CDF warns against interpretations of Church teaching that call homosexuality "neutral, or even good" (CHP 3), and it recognizes the need for authentic teaching:

> Special concern and pastoral attention should be directed toward those who have this condition, lest they be led to believe that the living out of this orientation in homosexual activity is a morally acceptable option. It is not (CHP 3).

It is not morally acceptable, in part, because it prevents people from participating in God's plan for humanity (see Answer 17), and it enslaves rather than frees them (see Answer 10). The CDF states, "As in every moral disorder, homosexual activity prevents one's own fulfillment and happiness by acting contrary to the creative wisdom of God. The Church, in rejecting erroneous opinions regarding homosexuality, does not limit but rather defends personal freedom and dignity realistically and authentically understood" (CHP 7).

The Church's call, then, is to love our neighbors as ourselves (Matt. 22:39; Mark 12:31). To love them as such is to will what is good for them and to hope for their salvation (see Answer 13). Thus, we must respectfully, compassionately, and sensitively teach them about the dangers of acting on same-sex attractions (see Answer 2), help them to overcome those desires (see Answer 18), and assist them in pleasing God in the way they live their lives.

Difficult for them as this may seem, it is not an impossible or even unrealistic proposition. Jesus said, "If any man would come after me, let him deny himself and take up his cross and follow me" (Matt. 16:24). The *Catechism*, acknowledging that a homosexual inclination is "a trial," instructs, "These persons are called to fulfill God's will in their lives. . . . By the virtues of self-mastery that teach them inner freedom, at times by the support of disinterested friendship, by prayer and sacramental grace, they can and should gradually and resolutely approach Christian perfection" (CCC 2358–2359; see also Answers 4, 18).

It is sometimes helpful to point out, as the CDF does, that the suffering one endures carrying his own cross may be seen as a reflection of the suffering Christ endured on his cross, and the two should be joined. People who suffer from same-sex attractions are called to carry out this joining:

Fundamentally, they are called to enact the will of God in their life by joining whatever sufferings and difficulties they experience in virtue of their condition to the sacrifice of the Lord's cross. That cross, for the believer, is a fruitful sacrifice since from that death come life and redemption. While any call to carry the cross or to understand a Christian's suffering in this way will predictably be met with bitter ridicule by some, it should be remembered that this is the way to eternal life for all who follow Christ (CHP 12).

Third, participate together in parish or diocesan programs geared toward helping people with same-sex attractions—but be vigilant that such programs are authentic! The CDF notes,

An authentic pastoral program will assist homo-sexual persons at all levels of the spiritual life: through the sacraments, and in particular through the frequent and sincere use of the sacrament of reconciliation, through prayer, witness, counsel, and individual care. In such a way, the entire Christian community can come to recognize its own call to assist its brothers and sisters, without deluding them or isolating them (CHP 15; see also Answer 20).

Fourth, EnCourage, a sister organization of Courage (see Answer 20), is a Catholic apostolate for family members and friends of loved one with same-sex attractions:

EnCourage helps members to focus on their own spiritual development with the goals of achieving peace and complete trust in God's Providence and his love for us and for the ones we love. EnCourage offers a supportive, confidential environment to share feelings, experiences, information, and guidance for maintaining healthy relationships with our loved ones with same-sex attractions (www.couragerc.org).

Finally, the Catholic Medical Association offers specific recommendations for ministries, bishops, priests, Catholic medical professionals, teachers, families, and others. See its document *Homosexuality and Hope* for more.

20. Where can a person with same-sex attractions go for more help?

Persons with same-sex attractions should know that they are not alone in their struggles. Help is offered from the individual level to the parish level, and from the diocesan level to the national level.

I recommend starting at the parish level to find out what programs are available through your local parish and diocese. Hopefully, you will find a chapter of Courage. The Courage apostolate is probably the most widespread organization today helping persons with same-sex attractions. It began within the Catholic Church and has always maintained good standing, even as it has spread internationally. The apostolate envisioned itself from the beginning as "a spiritual support system which would assist men and women with same-sex attractions in living chaste lives in fellowship, truth, and love" (www.couragerc.org). Additionally, "it has become a mainstream Catholic apostolate helping thousands of men and women find peace through fellowship, prayer, and the sacraments" (www.couragerc.org).

In addition to programs and ministries within the Church, good, orthodox Catholic therapists offer invaluable assistance to persons who are same sex-attracted and desire to live a life in keeping with Christ and his Church (see Answer 18). Check your local parish for possible referrals, as a reputation within the local Church might be the best way to find a therapist who is faithful to the magisterial teaching of the Church.

For additional assistance finding a therapist, there are at least two organizations that provide referrals nationwide in the United States. First, CatholicTherapists.com offers an easy-to-use online service for assistance in finding a local therapist. Note that although organizations such as this cannot guarantee the integrity of the therapists they refer, they do state that they "make the best effort to screen therapists for faithful adherence to Church teaching, by carefully reviewing their applications and references" (CatholicTherapists.com). Their mission, as they state it, "is to bring the healing love of Jesus Christ to those seeking psychological help and support. We provide psychological information and a list of counselors across the USA who are faithful to the teachings of the Catholic Church" (CatholicTherapists.com).

Another organization that provides referrals to therapists is the NARTH Institute. Its founders similarly state that they "make our best effort to screen all therapists to be sure they are licensed, ethical professionals" (narth.com), but there are no guarantees. NARTH is an acronym for National Association for the Research and Therapy of Homosexuality. The organization's website offers an abundance of additional resources.

The organizations mentioned above have good reputations for Catholic orthodoxy. Unfortunately, there are many other organizations that claim to be Catholic but are anything but orthodox in their teaching and approach to help. These groups attempt to give the impression that they represent all Catholics with same-sex attractions, but they truly represent only people who are ignorant of or outright dissent from Church teaching. They claim that authentic help such as that mentioned in this book is "homophobic" and discriminatory.

The CDF cautions against such organizations:

Increasing numbers of people today, even within the Church, are bringing enormous pressure to bear on the Church to accept the homosexual condition as though it were not disordered and to condone homosexual activity. Those within the Church who argue in this fashion often have close ties with those with similar views outside it. These latter groups are guided by a vision opposed to the truth about the human person, which is fully disclosed in the mystery of Christ. They reflect, even if not entirely consciously, a materialistic ideology which denies the transcendent nature of the human person as well as the supernatural vocation of every individual.

The Church's ministers must ensure that homosexual persons in their care will not be misled by this point of view, so profoundly opposed to the teaching of the Church. But the risk is great, and there are many who seek to create confusion regarding the Church's position and then to use that confusion to their own advantage (CHP 8).

A few such organizations to steer away from include Equally Blessed, Call to Action, DignityUSA, New Ways Ministry, and Fortunate Families. Additionally, watch out for parishes and schools identifying themselves as "LGBT friendly" and the like. Not only should serious Catholics sidestep these organizations, but we should be vigilant not to provide them any support. The CDF unambiguously states, "All support should be withdrawn from any organizations which seek to undermine the teaching of the Church, which are ambiguous about it, or which neglect it entirely" (CHP 17).

The Catholic Medical Association also recognizes the dangers of such organizations and exhorts Catholics to seek orthodox help:

> Support groups, therapists, and spiritual counselors who unequivocally support the Church's teaching are essential components of the help that is needed. Since the notions of sexuality in our country are so varied, patients seeking help must be cautious that the group or counselor supports Catholic moral imperatives (HH II:1).

Rest assured that if a person does his homework, he will find the help he needs: "It is very important for every Catholic experiencing same-sex attractions to know that there is hope, and that there is help" (HH II:1).

About the Author

Jim Blackburn is a Catholic apologist, speaker, and writer. He holds a master's degree in Theology from John Paul the Great Catholic University and is the author of the book *101 Quick Questions with Catholic Answers: Marriage, Divorce, and Annulment.* Jim supervised the Catholic Answers Q&A department for many years, and he remains a regular guest on the *Catholic Answers Live* radio program.

Become part of the team.
Help support Catholic Answers.

Catholic Answers is an apostolate dedicated to serving Christ by bringing the fullness of Catholic truth to the world. We help good Catholics become better Catholics, bring former Catholics "home," and lead non-Catholics into the fullness of the Faith.

Catholic Answers neither asks for nor receives financial support from any diocese. The majority of its annual income is in the form of donations from individual supporters like you.

To make a donation by phone using your credit card, please speak with one of our customer service representatives at 888-291-8000.

To make a donation by check, please send a check payable to "Catholic Answers" to:

> Catholic Answers
> 2020 Gillespie Way
> El Cajon, CA 92020

To make a donation online, visit **catholic.com**.

TO EXPLAIN & DEFEND THE FAITH

catholic.com